ENDANGERED
Animals of the Desert

TIME FOR KIDS

William B. Rice

Consultants

Timothy Rasinski, Ph.D.
Kent State University

Lori Oczkus
Literacy Consultant

Thorsten Pape
Animal Trainer

Based on writing from
TIME For Kids. *TIME For Kids* and the *TIME For Kids* logo are registered trademarks of TIME Inc. Used under license.

Publishing Credits

Dona Herweck Rice, *Editor-in-Chief*
Lee Aucoin, *Creative Director*
Jamey Acosta, *Senior Editor*
Heidi Fiedler, *Editor*
Lexa Hoang, *Designer*
Stephanie Reid, *Photo Editor*
Rachelle Cracchiolo, *M.S.Ed., Publisher*

Image Credits: pp.12–13, 20–21 Alamy;
p.26–27 Tourre Marc/Age Fotostock; p.33 (top)
The Bridgeman Art Library; p.57 (bottom) Corbis;
pp.40–41 Pablo Cáceres Contreras/Flickr; p.21
(bottom) Joseph Brandt/U.S. Fish and Wildlife
Service; p.22 (owl) John and Karen Hollingsworth/
US Fish and Wildlife Service; p.4, 17 (bottom),
22 (inset), 44–45 Getty Images; p.38 (bottom)
iStockphoto; pp.52–53, 53 (top & bottom) Lochman
Transparencies; p.46 Greg Neise/AFP/Getty
Images/Newscom; p.47 (left) Malcolm Schuyl/
FLPA Image Broker/Newscom; p.4 Cara Owsley
KRT/Newscom; p.43 Tui De Roy/Minden Pictures/
National Geographic Stock; pp.42–43 Maria
Stenzel/National Geographic Stock; p.54 National
Wildlife Federation; pp.8–9, 18, 19 (illustrations)
Timothy J. Bradley; p.9 (inset) Tom McHugh/
Photo Researchers, Inc.; pp.34–35 Superstock; p.57
(middle) University of Pennsylvania; p.56 IUCN.org;
p.41 (inset) Alvesgaspar/Wikipedia [CC-BY-SA]; p.54
Greenpeace.org; pp.50–51 Martybugs/Wikipedia;
p.57 (top) The White House Historical Association;
p.23 Hollingsworth, John and Karen/US Fish and
Wildlife Service; p.14 Steve Maslowski/U.S. Fish and
Wildlife Service; All other images from Shutterstock.

Teacher Created Materials

5301 Oceanus Drive
Huntington Beach, CA 92649-1030
http://www.tcmpub.com

ISBN 978-1-4333-4936-2
© 2013 Teacher Created Materials, Inc.

TABLE OF CONTENTS

DESERTED

Just imagine it. It's a new school year. There are hundreds of kids in the halls and classrooms. Every desk is taken. Teachers stand in each room. The principal greets everyone at the door. The secretary sits in the office. The custodian mops up a spill, and the librarian places books on the shelves.

As time passes, you notice empty desks here and there. Then, strangely, more and more are deserted. Your favorite teacher is missing. The principal is nowhere to be found. The spill is left unattended. Books are stacked in piles everywhere. Outside on the streets, things are eerily quiet, too. Where did everyone go?

And then you realize the horrible truth. People are dying off. There are fewer and fewer human beings. Your **species** is horribly **endangered**. You are among the very last of your kind. Will your species survive? Where did everyone go? And then you realize the truth. There are fewer and fewer humans. Your species is endangered, and you are among the last of your kind.

Humans are lucky. This isn't really happening. But around the world, animals are threatened. They face this scenario every day.

THINK LINK

- What animals call the desert their home?
- In what ways are they in danger?
- How can we help protect desert animals and their homes?

5

LIFE ON THE PLANET

We live in a beautiful world filled with life in many forms. Plants, animals, insects, and **fungi** all coexist. They all depend on each other.

A species is a type of life form. Tigers, blue whales, and willow trees are all types of species. There have been millions of species on Earth throughout history. They have lived over many hundreds of millions of years. They flourish in different ways at different times.

Humans are just one of millions of species on Earth.

Siberian tiger

maple tree

A Whole Lotta Critters!

Scientists estimate there are more than 1,700,000 kinds of **organisms** on Earth! Among them are more than 300,000 different kinds of plants, more than 60,000 kinds of animals, more than 1,000,000 kinds of insects, and more than 50,000 kinds of fungi, lichens, and similar organisms.

MASS EXTINCTIONS

Many big changes on Earth have caused a wide variety of life-forms to die off. Scientists think there have been at least five **mass extinctions** on Earth. Why did they happen? Some have been caused by a sudden worldwide **catastrophe**. For example, an asteroid may have struck Earth. Another cause may have been large, **sustained** volcanic eruptions around the world. Or there may have been a large fall in sea levels. Sustained global cooling or warming is also a likely cause.

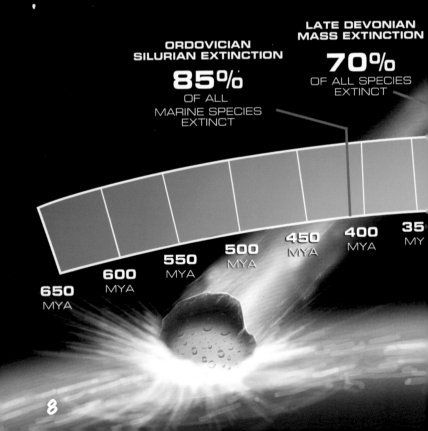

ORDOVICIAN
SILURIAN EXTINCTION

85%
OF ALL
MARINE SPECIES
EXTINCT

LATE DEVONIAN
MASS EXTINCTION

70%
OF ALL SPECIES
EXTINCT

650
MYA

600
MYA

550
MYA

500
MYA

450
MYA

400
MYA

35
MY

Back from the Dead

Can a species come back from the dead? Not really, but sometimes people get it wrong and think a species is extinct when it really isn't. The giant coelacanth fish was thought to have become extinct 65 million years ago. But in 1938, a living coelacanth was found off the South African coast. It is one of a handful of species thought to be extinct that was later found living.

coelacanth

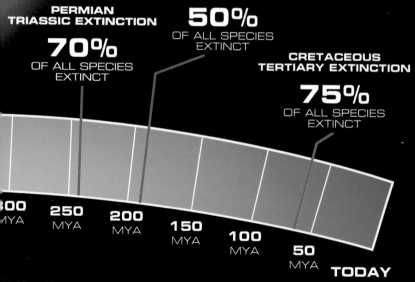

PERMIAN TRIASSIC EXTINCTION

70%
OF ALL SPECIES EXTINCT

TRIASSIC JURASSIC EXTINCTION

50%
OF ALL SPECIES EXTINCT

CRETACEOUS TERTIARY EXTINCTION

75%
OF ALL SPECIES EXTINCT

300 MYA   250 MYA   200 MYA   150 MYA   100 MYA   50 MYA   **TODAY**

(MYA = Millions of Years Ago)

ENDANGERED

Today, natural catastrophes don't seem to be the biggest danger to Earth's living things. Humans are. In fact, many animals such as the Cuban red macaw have become extinct from hunting or destruction of their **habitats**.

Many species have a high chance of becoming extinct. For now, they are endangered species. But they're in danger of being gone forever. There are always reasons for this. Nothing happens "just because." As scientists study animals, they try to decide two key things. Is extinction likely? And what will it take to make the species healthy again?

The majestic African mountain gorilla is at high risk of becoming extinct. It's among the many animals in the world that are endangered and should be protected.

10

red macaw

Local Extinction

When a species ceases to exist in an area in which it used to exist, but still exists elsewhere, it's called **extirpated**. Often, extirpation signals a warning that endangerment may be near, but not always. Sometimes, a local catastrophe causes extirpation. For example, some local species were wiped out when Mt. St. Helens erupted in 1980.

The gray wolf has been extirpated from many areas of the United States.

The Red List

There are many levels of endangerment and, therefore, many levels of concern. The International Union for **Conservation** of Nature and Natural Resources (IUCN) is a group dedicated to finding solutions to environmental problems. The IUCN has created categories of threats to species called the IUCN Red List of Threatened Species. Different threat levels offer different levels of protection to animals.

IUCN Red List

Extinct (EX)	Extinct in the Wild (EW)	Critically Endangered (CR)	Endangered (EN)	Vulnerable (VU)
No individuals of this species are living.	The only surviving individuals in this species are in captivity, or they exist only where relocated from their natural habitats.	In the wild, the species is at an extremely high risk of becoming extinct.	In the wild, the species has a very high risk of becoming extinct.	The species is at high risk of becoming extinct in the wild.

Threatened

The biggest risk is to threatened species. Threatened species are divided into these categories: critically endangered, endangered, and vulnerable. The IUCN and other organizations work hard to protect threatened species.

Near Threatened (NT)	Least Concern (LC)	Data Deficient (DD)	Not Evaluated (NE)
The species is likely to become endangered in the near future.	The species is at the lowest risk or no risk of endangerment. The species is widespread and abundant in the wild.	There is not enough data to determine the extinction risk for the species.	The species has not been evaluated for extinction or endangerment risk.

NORTH AMERICAN DESERTS

North America is home to some of the most beautiful deserts in the world. The Painted Desert in Arizona is known for its beautiful colors. Other deserts are admired for their unique flowers. Despite their beauty, these places aren't safe for the creatures that are under threat there.

Least Bell's vireo

Vireos are *insectivores*. These birds eat insects and bugs like grasshoppers, beetles, moths, and caterpillars. They can even pick the bugs off plants as they fly by.

LEAST BELL'S VIREO

At one time, this small songbird lived throughout California deserts. Now, few Least Bell's vireos survive to chirp their song. This tiny bird could nestle snuggly in a man's hand. But now it is in trouble from human development in its **territory**. With this loss and **encroachment** from larger cowbirds, the birds were disappearing. The good news? Human efforts are turning things around.

The cowbird is native to America's Great Plains, not to California. It came to California with the cows and dairies that were started there.

cowbird

Catching the Cowbirds

Cowbirds lay their eggs in vireo nests. The cowbird young are stronger and can push the vireo out of the nest. To help the vireo, people have built special cages to catch cowbirds.

MOJAVE DESERT TORTOISE

This shelled reptile is green to dark brown in color. The Mojave desert tortoise has sharp, claw-like scales on its front legs that can be used for digging. It carves out an underground burrow to escape the heat of summer and the cold of winter.

Mojave desert tortoises are in danger for many reasons. Mainly, they are being harmed by the loss of their habitat. They are also illegally captured as **exotic** pets. And disease is causing their **decline**. Their numbers have dropped by as much as 90 percent since the 1980s.

Turtle is a word used for all similarly shelled reptiles. Tortoise is the word for such reptiles that live on land.

Tortoise Facts

These tortoises grow to about 14 inches long and about 6 inches high, weighing up to 15 pounds. The tortoise is an herbivore, eating grasses, small plants, and cacti. Tortoises can survive a year or more without water! They also live from 80 to 100 years.

Tortoises spend almost all their time in their burrows. They hibernate in winter.

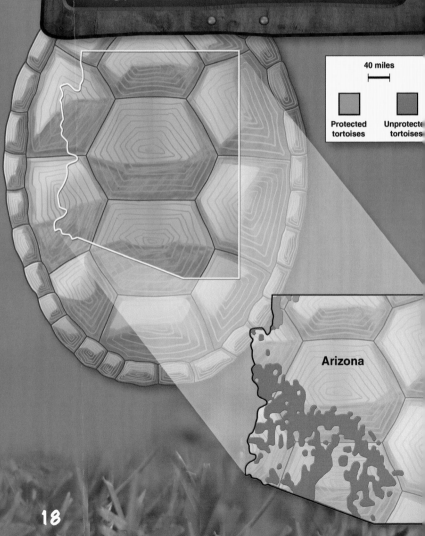

Threatened Tortoises

Mojave desert tortoises aren't the only tortoises in trouble. Many are facing extinction. **Activists** in Arizona's Sonoran desert are trying to protect the Sonoran desert tortoise. They are working to have the government take action and list the Sonoran desert tortoise as endangered. Some are already being protected.

40 miles

Protected tortoises

Unprotecte tortoises

Arizona

STOP! THINK...

- How large of an area does this map show?

- Where are the Sonoran desert tortoises located?

- Why do you think tortoises receive so much attention?

19

CALIFORNIA CONDOR

The California condor is the largest land bird in North America. Its wingspan is nearly 10 feet! Its feathers are mainly black, with white patches under its wings. And its head is bald.

The number of condors dropped in the 1900s. The bird almost became extinct due to **poaching**, poisoning, and habitat destruction. There were once only 22 condors left, all in captivity. There are now more than 380 condors. Nearly 200 of these birds are in the wild.

Depending on the condor's mood, the skin on the condor's head changes from yellow to bright red. This helps them communicate.

Poison Threats

Condors were threatened by two sources of poison. Lead poisoning came from the condors' food. When animals were shot and killed by humans but left behind, condors ate them—bullets and all. The lead from the bullets poisoned the condors. DDT was also a threat. It is a harmful **pesticide** that is no longer used because of its harsh consequences—but for a long time, it caused the death of many living things, including condors.

High Flying

Condors can fly up to 55 miles per hour and 15,000 feet high! They can also travel up to 160 miles per day, looking for food. Once in the air, condors can glide for hours without once flapping their wings.

Condors can live up to 60 years.

Condors make their nests on cliff ledges or high in caves.

MEXICAN SPOTTED OWL

Like most owls, the Mexican spotted owl is a **nocturnal** hunter. It perches above its prey. Then, it pounces down with its sharp talons.

The chestnut-and-white Mexican spotted owl is very rare. But the few that exist are spread over a huge area from Mexico to the northern United States. This bird is mainly threatened by habitat loss. Humans and other owl species are encroaching on its territory. This little owl is rapidly dying off. There are just over 2,000 of this once common bird living today.

Yuma Clapper Rail

The Yuma clapper rail is a bird that lives part of the year among the tidal marshes of the Colorado River. It makes its nest in the cattails and bulrushes of the wetlands. But it is endangered due to habitat loss. Humans have built dams that divert water, drying up the areas where the bird nests.

Habitat Loss

Humans, drought, and climate changes are destroying many old-growth forests—which are also a favorite environment for the Mexican spotted owl.

Most owls have yellow to red-orange eyes. Spotted owls are among the few with dark eyes.

23

AFRICAN DESERTS

Africa is filled with creatures that can't be found anywhere else on Earth. Unfortunately, too many of them are threatened. These animals need our help.

ADDAX

The **agile** addax is a type of antelope living in the Sahara desert. It is grayish brown or white, depending on the time of year. Its head has light patches that form an X over its nose. And there are two long, spiral horns above its eyes.

Hunting has endangered the addax. Its leather and meat are highly desired. Other threats include long droughts and habitat destruction. Scientists think there are fewer than 500 addaxes in the wild today.

Addaxes grow long, spiral horns that can be used for defense.

At one time, the addax was found throughout northern Africa and the Middle East. Today, they can only be found on a few remote sand dunes.

RHIM GAZELLE

The speedy rhim gazelle is found in remote areas of the Sahara desert. Its large hooves help it run quickly and easily in sand. It has a harder time running on firm ground. The gazelle is active in early morning and evening because of the desert heat. It gets most of its water from dew and the water in plants.

There are fewer than 2,500 rhim gazelles left in the wild. They're endangered because they have been hunted for sport. Their horns have become trophies for hunters. They're also losing its habitat to human development.

The rhim gazelle is also known as the *slender-horned gazelle*.

Species Stats

How do officials decide when a species is critically endangered, endangered, or vulnerable? They look at the numbers. When more than 90 percent of a species' population has been lost, it is considered critically endangered.

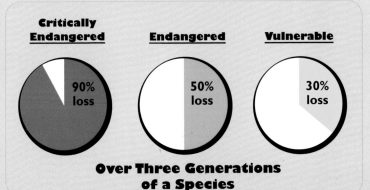

Critically Endangered

90% loss

Endangered

50% loss

Vulnerable

30% loss

Over Three Generations of a Species

The pale-tan coat of the rhim gazelle reflects the rays of the sun and keeps the animal cool.

Deserts in Danger

It's not just desert animals that are in danger of extinction. The deserts themselves are in danger. The biggest threat to deserts? Humans. Below are just some of the ways humans affect deserts.

Mining

Deserts are home to plants and animals as well as precious resources such as oil and gold. Mining can damage the land with poisonous chemicals.

Nuclear Waste

Because they are so isolated, deserts have been used as test areas for **nuclear weapons**. The waste from these tests has damaged the plants, the animals, and the soil in these deserts.

Development

As the human population grows, we look to new areas to make our homes. Buildings and concrete may replace desert sands. Thriving deserts can quickly become nearly lifeless.

Off-Road Vehicles

People are eager to explore these beautiful lands. But when off-road vehicles drive off marked paths, they can kill desert weeds and small plants that protect the soil. This small green layer is important to the desert **ecosystem** and can take a long time to regrow if damaged.

BLACK RHINOCEROSES

The black rhinoceros is really gray, brown, or even white in color. Its big body is nearly 3,000 pounds and 12 feet long! Huge numbers of the rhino once roamed southern Africa. Sadly, there are only about 4,000 still living.

The rhino has become endangered because of poaching. Its horns are in high demand for use as knife handles and art. Some people believe they have power as medicine, too.

Coming Back!

The southern white rhinoceros is the only rhino to recover from near extinction. In the early 1900s, there were less than 20 white rhinos. Protection and conservation efforts have increased its numbers to about 20,000!

The black rhino, also called the *hook-lipped rhino*, has a hooked upper lip that it uses like a hand to help grab food!

Crafty Conservationists

How do you keep poachers from poaching? What about cutting off the horns before they can do it? Some conservationists are using **tranquilizer** darts to put rhinos to sleep. Then, the conservationists cut off the animal's horns. The rhinos live—and no poachers kill them because the horns are gone. It may not be the best solution, but it is helping rhino populations increase.

CHEETAH

The cheetah is a large member of the cat family. Its speed and agility make it a fast runner and a fierce hunter. But it's in danger now. Over time, it has lost habitat land to human development. It's losing its prey for the same reason. No food means no cheetahs. Cheetah cubs are especially vulnerable. Only about 10 percent of cubs live more than a few weeks. They are often hunted by predators.

The cheetah is the fastest animal on land, running up to 75 miles per hour over short distances. It can accelerate from 0 to 60 miles per hour in 3 seconds!

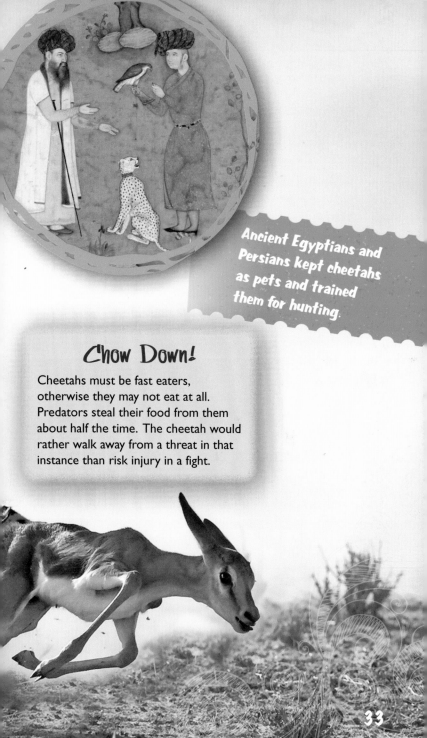

Chow Down!

Cheetahs must be fast eaters, otherwise they may not eat at all. Predators steal their food from them about half the time. The cheetah would rather walk away from a threat in that instance than risk injury in a fight.

ASIAN DESERTS

The deserts of Asia are wild, windblown stretches of land. Visitors are impressed by the amazing views—and the amazing animals—they find there. Unfortunately, too many of these animals face extinction.

The takhi horse is a little more than 50 inches tall and about 7 feet long. It weighs about 650 pounds.

The takhi is considered the last of the wild horses.

TAKHI

The takhi is a rare type of wild horse. It lives in areas of central Asia. At one time, it was extinct in the wild. But it has been returned to its native habitat.

There were once only 31 takhi in captivity. Today, there are just over 1,500 of them, with 250 of those in the wild. All the takhi today are **descendants** of those that were in captivity.

The takhi is also called Przewalski's horse. *Takhi* is its Mongolian name, which means "holy."

WILD BACTRIAN CAMEL

The Bactrian camel is one of two types of camels in the world. It's known by the two humps on its back, and it's native to central Asia.

Camels have been **domesticated** for thousands of years. They have mainly been used as beasts of burden to carry people and goods. But some camels live in the wild. Today, there are only about 950 wild camels. They have been hunted heavily for both their hide and meat. They also must compete with other animals for water and plants to eat.

The wild camel can survive by drinking saltwater with even more salt than seawater! Domesticated camels cannot tolerate the saltwater.

Protection

The camel's thick eyelashes help protect its eyes from the common sandstorms where it lives. It's also able to narrow its nostrils into slits to keep out sand.

The wild Bactrian camel is among the world's rarest mammals.

This camel lives in some of the most extreme conditions in the world. It survives frigid winters and extremely hot summers.

ARABIAN ORYX

The Arabian oryx has a white coat and large black stripes on its neck and head. It has the amazing ability to detect when rain is coming and move toward it. In the wild, it covers huge areas of land to satisfy its thirst.

By the early 1970s, the oryx was nearly hunted to extinction. People have helped increase its numbers. Today, it lives in the wild again.

The Arabian oryx is also called the white oryx.

The Arabian oryx has long, slightly curved horns up to 30 inches in length.

The Arabian oryx was the first animal to receive vulnerable status again after being labeled extinct in the wild. There are more than 1,000 of these animals now in the wild and more than 6,000 in captivity.

SOUTH AMERICAN DESERTS

South America is home to some of the driest places on Earth. Sadly, these unique areas are losing some of their most interesting animals. These animals are under threat.

The Chilean Woodstar has always had limited distribution, which means it has lived in a relatively small area. That fact adds to its vulnerability today.

CHILEAN WOODSTAR

The Chilean Woodstar is the smallest bird in Chile. It is a type of hummingbird. It is only about three inches long with a short, slender beak.

Like so many other endangered animals, it is in danger from habitat loss. Much of its native land has been taken over for farming. It is thought that only about 1,200 of these tiny birds exist today.

Poisoned!

Pesticides are chemicals used by farmers to control insects and other pests that are harmful to plants. In the 1960s, an influx of Mediterranean fruit flies caused a lot of worry for farmers. But the pesticide that was used to stop them also probably endangered the Chilean Woodstar.

fruit fly

HUEMUL

The huemul lives in the Andes. Its sturdy body and short legs make it well suited to the harsh terrain. Once very common, there are now very few huemuls. They are losing their native habitat. They are also in danger from poachers and non-native animals that eat their food. Non-native species may also be the reason why huemuls are having fewer young and dying sooner than before.

The huemul is also known as the *South Andean deer*.

Shrinking Families

In the past, huemuls lived in groups as large as 100. Today, groups may be as small as two or three huemuls.

The huemul is shown on Chile's national coat of arms.

POR LA RAZON O LA FUERZA

Taruca

The taruca is very much like the huemul, only it lives in the northern mountains. It is also called the *North Andean deer*.

43

ANDEAN MOUNTAIN CAT

This small wild cat lives in the Andes Mountains. Fewer than 2,500 of them are thought to exist. The cat is silvery gray with dark spots and stripes. It is like a smaller version of the snow leopard. The cat is endangered because its habitat has **deteriorated**. The cats that remain are living farther away from one another. But species that live together in large numbers survive better than those that are divided.

The Andean mountain cat is very rare, and little is known about it. Much of what we know has been learned from its hide, for which it has often been killed.

Chinchillas

The chinchilla has long been hunted for its fur. As one of the main sources of food for the Andean mountain cat, its reduced numbers have created a limited food supply for the cat.

Competition

The pampas cat is a cat that lives in the same area as the Andean mountain cat. It hunts and lives in much the same way. The cats compete with one another for survival. They are almost in a daily race to live.

AUSTRALIAN DESERTS

Australia is known for its beautiful coasts and also for its vast remote outback. Life down under isn't easy. Some animals there are in serious trouble.

The woylie is a distant cousin of the kangaroo and likewise carries its babies, or joeys, in a pouch.

WOYLIE

The woylie once lived in nearly all of Australia. Now, it is found in only three small areas that cover less than one percent of the land. There are about 6,000 woylies now.

After being named an endangered species, the woylie's numbers rose to more than 40,000. But then its numbers dropped again. Sickness may have been the cause. The woylie is in danger today because of habitat loss from farming. Non-native species, such as the red fox, also hunt the woylie for food.

Digging for Food

The woylie has an unusual diet for a mammal. It may eat plants, seeds, and insects, but mainly it eats underground fungi. It digs out the fungi with its strong claws.

red fox

YAMINON

The yaminon once lived throughout Australia. It now lives in a very small area. There may be just over 100 in existence. Wild dogs are eating them. The yaminon habitat has been taken over by non-native grass. Its food source is disappearing. So is the yaminon.

The yaminon is about 3 feet long and weighs 70 pounds.

The yaminon uses its long, strong claws to burrow. Its pouch opens downward to protect its young from all the digging and dirt.

The yaminon is also called the northern hairy-nosed wombat.

The Nose Knows

The yaminon's nose is important to its survival. It has very poor eyesight, so it smells its food in the dark.

49

NUMBAT

The pointy-faced, bushy-tailed numbat once lived throughout most of Australia. Now, it lives in just a few tiny areas. Only two groups of numbats exist in the wild. The European red fox was released into the Australian wild in the 1800s. Since then, the fox has hunted the numbat and endangered it. Fires have also threatened the numbat. Conservation is bringing it back, though. And the numbat serves as the official animal of Western Australia.

The numbat is small and gray or reddish brown in color. It is about 18 inches long, including its tail, and weighs a little over a pound.

The numbat mainly eats termites with its long, sticky tongue. It can eat up to 20,000 termites a day!

Beware!

Non-native species almost always harm the natural environment of an area. Non-native plants and animals should never be introduced because of the harm they do to native life-forms.

European red fox

51

DJOONGARI

The djoongari once lived in most of Western Australia. But Europeans in the 1800s brought in non-native animals such as cats and foxes. The djoongari was soon in danger. Farming and cattle took over much of its habitat. It is now found only in a few small places. Through conservation, the animal has risen to the vulnerable level. Public access to these creatures is limited. This helps protect them from curious or careless observers.

The heavily whiskered djoongari is also called the *Shark Bay mouse*.

The djoongari eats flowers and plants but also insects and spiders when its favorite food, flowers, aren't available.

These little animals like to live in sand dunes at the base of cliffs. They make tunnels and trails in the vegetation to get around easily.

Shark Bay mouse paw ›

A HELPING HAND

Is there anything you can do to help endangered animals? Should you even try? The answer to both questions is yes. We know that species are related to one another. If one falls, many others are affected. That includes people, too! If people do something that harms a species, then the balance of nature is destroyed. And people harm themselves in the process.

The National Wildlife Federation is one of many organizations that work to protect animals.

Help Out

Talk with your family about organizations (such as the one above) that work to protect the environment and help threatened and endangered animals recover. Contact the organizations to see how you can help.

GREENPEACE

So what can YOU do?

Protect the Environment

Always remember the three Rs—reduce, reuse, and recycle. Practicing the three Rs goes a long way to help the environment and animal species.

Protect Habitats

You can plant flowers to attract bees or put up a birdhouse with bird food to help your local birds.

Who's Making a Difference?

Many people around the world are working to protect endangered species and their environments. Some were early heroes of the movement. Others are still leading the way today. Learn who they are—and maybe you'll want to join them, too!

International Union for Conservation of Nature and Natural Resources (IUCN)

This international organization focuses on finding solutions to pressing environmental challenges. It publishes the IUCN Red List of Threatened Species, which lists the world's endangered species. The IUCN supports scientific research around the world. It also brings together governments to develop ways to solve the challenges facing the environment and its species.

Making a Difference

Theodore Roosevelt

President Theodore Roosevelt had a great appreciation for nature. He became increasingly alarmed by the damage being done to land and wildlife. As president, he created the United States Forest Service and established 51 federal bird reservations, 4 national game preserves, 150 national forests, and 5 national parks. He also protected about 230 million acres of public land. He is remembered by many as the conservationist president.

Loren Corey Eiseley

Loren Corey Eiseley was a professor who taught at several universities in the 20th century. He studied and wrote about many things, including science and nature. He was a popular writer who helped influence public opinion. His deep appreciation for the environment is evident in his work.

Aldo Leopold

Aldo Leopold was a professor and author. He is best known for his book *A Sand County Almanac*, which is a collection of essays that advocates responsibility between people and the land they live on. This book has sold more than two million copies. Leopold was very influential in creating **environmental ethics** and preserving wilderness areas. He emphasized the importance of **biodiversity** and the importance of looking at ecosystems as a whole.

GLOSSARY

activists—people who take action for political purposes

agile—quick and well-coordinated

biodiversity—the variation of life types within a given area, such as an ecosystem, biome, or planet

catastrophe—a large and terrible event with harmful consequences

conservation—the protection of plant and animal species and the environment

decline—decrease in number

descendants—the children, grandchildren, great-grandchildren, and so on of a person or animal

deteriorated—worsened or lessened in value

domesticated—raised to live peacefully with people, usually for their service

ecosystem—all the plants, animals, and other elements of a particular area

encroachment—the invasion of another's territory

endangered—threatened and at risk of extinction

environmental ethics—moral reasons for protecting the environment

exotic—foreign to a particular area

extirpated—extinct within a local area while still existing elsewhere

fungi—group of organisms that include mushrooms, molds, and yeasts

habitats—natural living environments

insectivores—animals that eat insects

mass extinction—a dramatic decrease and widespread dying off of many species of animals and plants over a very large area of the planet

native—naturally belonging to an area

nocturnal—active at night

nuclear weapons—extremely powerful explosive devices

organisms—living things

pesticide—a substance used to destroy pests

poaching—illegal killing of an animal, usually for some financial gain

species—a specific animal group with common characteristics

sustained—ongoing continuously

territory—an area that an animal or group of animals uses and defends

tranquilizer—a drug used to reduce anxiety and muscle activity

INDEX

BIBLIOGRAPHY

Bradley, Timothy. *Danger in the Desert.* **Teacher Created Materials, 2012.**

Life in Earth's deserts pushes life to the edge of survival. The desert is an unforgiving, hostile environment. Every single drop of water is precious. Meet the amazing desert plants and animals that won't waste a drop. They never know if it might be their last.

Mackay, Richard. *The Atlas of Endangered Species: Revised and Updated.* **University of California Press, 2008.**

It's scary to think that Earth may lose 20 percent of its species by 2030. This book takes an in-depth look at many of the ecosystems that are affected by this scary statistic. You will find lots of colorful maps and detailed photographs.

Radley, Gail. *Vanishing from Grasslands and Deserts.* **Carolrhoda Books, 2001.**

Discover more about 10 desert creatures whose lives are in danger. Explore each creature through an essay, key fact, poem, and realistic illustration. You'll even learn what's being done to help these precious animals.

Wright, Alexandra. *Will We Miss Them? Endangered Species.* **Charlesbridge Publishing Incorporated, 1991.**

Through beautiful paintings and intimate poems, you'll meet 21 endangered and threatened animals. You'll also find activities to do at home and organizations you can support.

MORE TO EXPLORE

World Wildlife Fund
http://www.worldwildlife.org/species

Find out what the World Wildlife Fund is doing to protect many of Earth's endangered animals. You'll find lots of information about each animal at this site.

Earth's Endangered Creatures
http://www.earthsendangered.com

Just how many creatures are on the endangered species list? This site has a list of every endangered animal. You can search alphabetically by name, world region, or type of animal, such as mammal.

Numbat
http://www.perthzoo.wa.gov.au/animals-plants/australia/australian-bushwalk/numbat

Are you curious to find out more about numbats? The Perth Zoo's website has plenty of facts about these cute little critters. You can watch baby numbats being hand-fed and see a collection of up-close images of the orphaned numbats.

Wild Bactrian Camel
http://www.arkive.org/wild-bactrian-camel/camelus-ferus

The wild Bactrian camel is critically endangered. Here, you'll learn more about this fascinating, rare animal through photographs and information about their habitat, the threats they face, and conservation efforts.

ABOUT THE AUTHOR

William B. Rice grew up in Pomona, California and graduated from Idaho State University with a degree in geology. He works at a California state agency that strives to protect the quality of surface and groundwater resources. Protecting and preserving the environment is important to him. William is married with two children and lives in Southern California.